WHAT IF YOU KNEW?

A revolutionary approach to regaining your health and life.

KYLE DAIGLE, DC

Intended Use Statement

The content of this book is intended for information purposes only. The medical information in this book is intended as general information only and should not be used in any way to diagnose, treat, cure, or prevent disease. The goal of the book is to present information and offer suggestions for nutritional support and health maintenance.

It is the sole responsibility of the user of this information to comply with all local and federal laws regarding the use of such information, as it relates to the scope and type of the user's practice.

Disclaimers

This book is not intended as a substitute for the medical advice of physicians. The reader should regularly consult a physician in matters relating to his/her health and particularly with respect to any symptoms that may require diagnosis or medical attention.

The information in this book is meant to supplement, not replace, proper (name your sport) training. Like any sport involving speed, equipment, balance and environmental factors, (this sport) poses some inherent risk. The authors and publisher advise readers to take full responsibility for their safety and know their limits. Before practicing the skills described in this book, be sure that your equipment is well maintained, and do not take risks beyond your level of experience, aptitude, training, and comfort level

Although the author and publisher have made every effort to ensure that the information in this book was correct at press time, the author and publisher do not assume and hereby disclaim any liability to any party for any loss, damage, or disruption caused by errors or omissions, whether such errors or omissions result from negligence, accident, or any other cause.

Financial Disclosure

Dr. Kyle Daigle is a board member of SNA Technologies and has ownership interest in SNA Technologies.

He is also a distributor for Juice Plus. He has no ownership interest in Juice Plus but does receive commission off sales of products.

DEDICATION

I would like to dedicate this book to my wife, Alexa, and to my daughter, Blakesly, for their continued support. Developing this book, as a current student, active healthcare professional, and board member of developing software program has meant many long hours, hotels, various road trips, and business meetings all over the country.

I also want to dedicate this book to the readers. This is valuable information that can help change your life.

Third, my patients, thank you for the love and support over the years. Thank you for teaching me so much neurology.

Lastly, my parents, I love you and so grateful for the support and guidance throughout my education.

Contents

ABOUT THE AUTHOR
Kyle Daigle, DC

D
r. Kyle Daigle is an alternative healthcare practitioner. Dr. Daigle joined SNA Technologies in December 2014 as President, Chief Medical Officer, and Managing Director for SNA Global. He is the co-inventor of U.S. Patent Pending Neurosage and has Intellectual Property with Systemic Neural Adaptation. Currently, Dr. Daigle owns and operates a successful clinical practice, Ultimate Performance Chiro & Rehab in Lake Charles, Louisiana. Dr. Daigle played college baseball at McNeese State University where he was a member of the 2006 Southland Conference Championship team. After leaving McNeese, Dr. Daigle continued his education at LSU where he studied Biological Science. While at LSU, Dr. Daigle worked as a research assistant in the Pennington Biomedical Research Center. Dr. Daigle is a current member of The International Association of Functional Neurology and Rehabilitation. Dr. Daigle is an Alumni of Parker University. While at Parker University, Dr. Daigle was the nutrition club President. Dr. Daigle continues to pursue clinical research in the field of kinesiology, functional medicine, virtual reality, digital therapeutics, and functional neurology.

CHAPTER 1:

Introduction

The brain is one of the most crucial organs for us to survive in life. It controls every vital function from our breathing, digestion, detoxification, circulation, endocrine, lymphatic and motor control. Stimulation is what drives the development of the brain from childbirth extending into our Silver sneaker years. Each muscle, every movement, every touch, taste, smell, sight, and hear all stimulates and drives the function of the development of this intricate system.

In America, we see childhood obesity and chronic diseases like Diabetes sky rocket at an exponential rate. Why? Well, for starters the American people are succumbing to conformity, where everyone does what everyone else does. Albert Einstein has called insanity "doing the same thing repeatedly, and expecting a different result." We need to change, whether it be our daily routine, our lack of movement, physical and social interaction, spiritual life, and even mental outlook to break this vicious cycle. We get too caught up in the modern world that we forget the basic needs for survival. I see kids in my current practice that look like zombies, physically attached to their iPad, iPhone, smart phones, and fidget spinners. Parents are running from all ends trying to meet the demands of parenthood, which causes them to start selecting foods such as microwaveable dinners or fast food chains because of the ease of convenience.

Convenience plus conformity equals the rise of our chronic diseases and potentially has some contribution to behavioral and academic problems. As I mentioned, the brain is one of the most crucial organs for us to survive in life. Imagine if the brain was not getting its proper nutrients to function on a daily, monthly basis, and annual basis, even into decades because of a lack of education on healthy eating. **We have a dietary lifestyle that has become detachment from our primitive ancestors**. We are eating things, which have the word artificial (which I believe means fake) into our DAILY diets. In my undergraduate days, I worked at a biomedical research center called Pennington Biomedical in Baton Rouge. I was awakened to what is going on with our healthcare problems. I was a biology student at LSU eagerly studying to get into Medical School, studying and reading biology, organic chemistry, physics, mathematics, and even psychology. I was the typical college student, stayed up late all night drinking caffeinated drinks and energy drinks, eating convenient, fast foods and frequently sick with allergies and low energy. As I am sitting down at the table during my lunch break, it hits me while eating this McDonald hamburger that contains various preservatives and artificial ingredients. Could this be the reason why I feel like I do?

I went home that night and started doing my research on how to build the immune system. The more I read, the stronger the evidence was that the gastrointestinal tract is significant. Did you know that up to 60-80% of our immune system is colonized in our gastrointestinal tract? You would think that Probiotics, digestive enzymes, essential fatty acid, alkaline forming foods, and cave man like diets could be the answer to all these chronic health problems. Have you heard of the acronym KISS? Keep it so simple! Let's break down the word chronic. Chronic means that it takes some duration whereas acute is short term. So, if we have a chronic disease, this is something that has been perpetuation the immune system for some time. The next question is WHY? So, if we chronically live the American lifestyle, stressed, sedentary, artificial foods, stay dehydrated because we prefer a carbonated drink than water because of the taste daily for months and even years, that this could be a contributing factor to our Chronic Diseases lifestyles. Look around! It's everywhere, Mr. Jones finally got diagnosed with diabetes while his hairs on his legs have been falling off for years, and Mrs. Jones finally got diagnosed with Parkinson's after she has been having stomach pains and digestive issues for ten years plus.

In my opinion, this is one of the possible answers, and it's what we are eating and not moving that is causing a rise in neurological and chronic diseased lifestyles. **We have aborted the lifestyle that God intended us to live**, by not enjoying all the sights and sceneries he designed for our viewing. Instead, we sit home in our chairs while we watch reality television shows, scroll on Facebook and Instagram on our smart phones wishing we could live our lives like everyone else. God intended you to live: be happy, be thankful, and to help others. How can you do this when you are in chronic pain, can't go out and enjoy a run because you must be close to a bathroom, can't walk down the boardwalk because your feet feel likes pins and needles when you walk. **God created a bountiful pharmacy of vital minerals and nutrients that nourish our immune system, support our brain, organs, and joints**. But, you aren't going to get them in your artificial meals, fast food, and carbonated sugary drinks.

When you wake up to this idea, that you need a reality check to get your health back. You will join the movement of thousands that are reclaiming their God given lifestyle and potential back! You eat the foods that God provided for you such as what he created, not what some scientist put together in a lab, or some factory designed your food into some animal like shape. Once you start to develop more energy, you start wanting to move more. Movement is what drives the brain giving you more life, more reasons to travel and enjoy what we were all designed to do, be grateful!

This book is a self-educated approach to teaching you how to regain your life purpose, reclaim our health, and catapult your happiness.

CHAPTER 2:

Diet

The standard American diet consists of highly refined carbohydrates, artificial flavorings and foods, synthetic sugars, preservatives, genetically modified, and food dyes all which in my opinion plays a contribution to our health problems. It's nonsense to think that diet isn't that important. I have local doctors in my area that tell patients that I practice an "unorthodox way." It baffles me that people simply do not have any standard education on diet and lifestyle. **That same pill goes to the same place your food does, so if you consistently eat depleted nutrient meals with all these artificial ingredients and chemicals that it couldn't even cause a little inflammation (stress on your body.)** Imagine trying to digest food that has been chemically altered or even artificial. You wouldn't think that it could even require a little extra energy to digest and detoxify this from your body? People are only not eating food they are eating food like substances. Watch Food Matters, Food Inc., Hungry for A Change, Forks over Knives if you don't believe me. These guys are trying to educate the public on how to eat, and it all starts with your weekly or monthly trip to the grocery store. That is the most important trip you can make besides going to a weekly worship session or church. Food does matter, just like your medication is important! We need to break this vicious mindset of I will one day eat right, or I will just start my diet tomorrow or Monday.

It's time to wake up! You need to start now, today, this very instance! You need to get rid of the diet drinks, toss the synthetic sugary energy drinks, avoid that fast food restaurant for lunch or dinner, and get rid of your microwavable dinners. Go to the grocery store and start shopping on the outside aisles. **Eat real food, food that your ancestors would have eaten 100 plus years ago.** Would they eat a candy bar or drink some drink that looks like acid? No! They would eat vegetables from their garden, meat from the fields or their hunts, fruit from their trees, and drink fresh water when able to find it.

What makes any difference between the two ages of our humanity? We have become so far advanced that we are starting to lose the basic universal education for immediate survival. **We go daily, monthly, yearly without even consuming a daily value of nutrients because our foods are depleted of minerals**, or they just have ingredients in them that you would find in a chemical lab. **Google the ingredients in the foods you are eating.** It's scary what you will find, I mean I would just like to eat an apple, but then you see this apple in a canned jar has all these big fancy chemical words in it. What in the world? High Fructose Corn Syrup[1], Aspartame[2], Genetically Modified[3], Enriched with Cyanocobalamin, or even Phosphoric Acid[4]. Holy crap, Acid? Why in the world would I want to put Phosphoric Acid in my body? Phosphoric Acid can be found as a rust converter, fertilizing feedstock, a component of home cleaning products, and your sugary carbonated drink. People put this stuff in their bodies daily without even understanding what it's doing to our intestinal lining, or detoxification, and even our bones.

Think about this, how many carbonated drinks do you consume daily? Most of my patients tell me they drink 1-3 sodas a day. Do you know how much sugar and chemicals are in these drinks? Start calculating your sugar intake! Most of them who drink 1-3 sodas don't even take a vitamin. **They don't even eat a single serving of fruits or vegetables. They consume mostly artificial fake food throughout the day, with a drink loaded with preservatives and synthetic sugars.** People don't get rid of toxins as they should due to the accumulation of so many of them all at once compacted in your drinks and foods, and have you seen all the nutrients needed to help assist in detoxification of your body? Just to rattle off a few: B Vitamins, Glutathione, Magnesium, Glycine, Vitamin C, Choline, and Glutamine. If you don't consume these in a supplement or foods that possess these nutrients and vitamins, looks like you're not going to be able to detoxify your diet drinks, artificial foods, and potentially even pharmaceuticals. I do believe in genetic testing for liver detoxification; you should ask your doctor to check your Cytochrome P450s and liver markers to see even if you can metabolize the drugs you are on.

So, you may end up getting some major acid reflux after you eat your fried food, hamburgers, and 12 pack of iced cold beer. You may end up having to rush to the bathroom, following eating some pizza, pasta, or bowl of cereal. You may end up breaking out with red splotches everywhere after you dip your sushi in some soy sauce and even start itching on your palms or feet. Your child may be battling eczema so bad, that when they open their hands, they bleed from being so dry. Your child may be having behavior or academic problems in school that could be related to a sensitivity of food dyes[6] or unknown food allergies or senitivities[7]. I have personally witnessed these symptoms in my practice significantly reduce with proper education on an "Anti-inflammatory diet, Paleo Diet, Blood type Diet, Low Carbohydrate, Specific Carbohydrate Diet, Ketogenic, Gluten and Dairy free diet[8].

Diet! Which one works best for me? If you haven't read eating per your blood type, then that is a great start. I personally try to stick to a Paleo diet: meats, fruit, vegetables, little to no grain, and occasional nuts. Meats are a tough one because of the processing and packaging, and they load it up with various chemicals or additives. When purchasing meat, try to buy grass fed meat if possible, free range, local and organic. Fresh vegetables and fruit are highly recommended, organic if possible and try to avoid GMO's.

Gluten and Diary free diets are also beneficial in most cases9. I have patients tell me Jesus ate bread and broke it for his disciples. Yes, he did! But they also didn't spray round up and other fertilizers on the wheat either. People spray these vegetables and fruit down with a suit that looks like you're going into a quarantine section of an infectious disease lab. Could the chemicals from the pesticide and fertilization possibly get inside the fruit? You know how many topical creams are out there: you can get rid of a rash and increase hormone level with creams. So, you think a fruit or vegetable skin will block the chemicals from getting embedded in the fruit? That's why I tell people to eat organic as much as possible. Then you have the Anti-Organic, Anti-vegetable, and Anti-Fruit person who says that's why I just don't eat vegetables and fruit to stay away from all those chemicals. While they are neglecting to realize, their typical diet is nothing but artificial, loaded with insane amounts of toxins, and even carcinogens (chemicals that are known to cause cancer). It's a double edge sword! I have seen kids have high levels of **Arsenic** in their blood. Where do you think that comes from? **Watch what you eat!**

When I was in Chiropractic school in Dallas, I had a Biochemistry Professor Dr. Sarkar ask "Kyle why didn't you consider becoming a medical doctor?" My reply to him was I did until I understood Biochemisty (the chemical system of your body) and how the brain functions, then I could effectively help patients out. Which is why I have a successful clinical practice. If you are in the medical industry, I commend you for all the hard work you have spent in school. I hope you take no offense to this book but it's hard to treat someone with all these medications when the foundation isn't there. Our patients are sick, they are deprived of nutrients and vitamins, and most of them dehydrated. When we start putting them on all these medications, **without ruling out any of these underlying factors like Vitamin D deficiencies, Digestive Disorders, Inflammation, Thyroid, Cardiovascular, Food allergies/sensitivities, environmental triggers, and muscle imbalances no wonder they have some many issues.**

As I write part of this book, I am in New Orleans waiting on watching my favorite college football team play LSU. This morning, I was in the restaurant at the hotel, and I just looked around at the table for breakfast, and I see a big part of the problem. I see kids eating cereal loaded with food dyes and synthetic sugar, people eating more bread than they should, drinking Cokes and artificial food. Just because everyone else feeds their kids Fruit Loops, Powered Donuts, Pop Tarts, and Toast doesn't mean you must do the same. My little daughter looks like she had been in a food fight, has blue berries and strawberries all over her face and hands. Do I think I am better than everyone else? No, but I am a little educated when it comes to common sense nutrition. **Eat real food, eat nutrient rich food, and eat like you would have 200 years ago.**

My wife loves to shop, so we decided to make a trip to the Riverwalk in New Orleans. After going to a couple of shoe stores, we decided it was time to eat lunch. It's hard to eat clean when traveling, especially in a mall food court. As we are sitting down, I again decided to just people watch at what people are eating. I'm sure you could guess what they are eating, but it is hamburgers, French fries, chicken nuggets, fried shrimp, and burritos. I told my beautiful wife that our table looks like we are eating rabbit food compared to the hundreds of people around us. The guy next to us was griping about how nasty the bathroom was. He said that the insulin shot bin was almost overflowing. Then, I watched a lady who was so morbidly obese, chowing down on a 20-piece chicken nugget, large size French fries and 32 oz. Diet Coke. As I am looking at her, she took a handful of pills with her coke, my wife nudges me and says Kyle, quit staring. I wanted to walk up to the table and give this lady a reality check, but I didn't. I could barely eat my salad, and she's over here eating like a she has the munchies. Ever wonder why someone can eat a Family Sized Bar-B-Que Chips but can barely finish off a bowl of fruit or a large salad? **It's because there is so little nutrition in poor quality processed food in comparison to that real God given fruit and vegetable plate. We need to eat for nutrients, not for Calories.**

While I was researching fast food chains, I came across an article that stated there were around 22 restaurants located within a hospital[10]. Talk about Sick Care instead of Health Care[11]. Why would a hospital allow this to be affiliated with their business? Could be a great partnership. Might as well toss in a brewery and a smoke shop. Then, you see a picture of a little child who appears to have cancer eating an ice cream cone[12]. Are you kidding me? Who fed this kid ice cream? Did you know that sugar feeds the growth of cancer cells and suppresses the immune system[13]? I don't think a kid who just went thru some chemo or radiation should be eating something that can make cancer grow, but that's just my unorthodox thinking. I once read an article that stated chemo and radiation do not only kill cancer cells it also suppresses the immune system. If the immune system controls our ability to fight infections, wouldn't you want to take something that also bolsters it? I would much rather go to battle with an arsenal of ammunition than a handful of pillows.

The Environmental Working Group studied the umbilical cord blood of 10 babies, an average of 237 chemical toxins were found[14]. I presented a health talk at the VA hospital in Dallas Texas to the nursing and doctors about nutrition, I mentioned this study after a Medical Doctor questioned me over how do young kids get cancer. For a developing child, the immune system and organs are being exposed to an incredible number of chemicals.

ABC or NBC News tomorrow will probably mention something about Vitamin C may help cancer treatment study finds[15]. Eating blue berries produces a nutrient called Ellagic acid that induces suicide in cancer cells[16]. Drinking lemons may help increase the glutathione levels in your liver helping you to detoxify more efficiently. This is great information, but do we use it? Imagine trying to eat all the most nutrient rich foods like a super food Goji Berry or Acai. I bet this will help you recover faster by trying to nourish your immune system and body. **Feed it, and feed it the good REAL stuff**. If you ever take a trip to an All-Inclusive resort in Mexico, go to the weight room or the spa, and they have chlorophyll water to drink.

Drink it up! I love that stuff! Chlorophyll is blood purification nutrient17, so add that to your daily regimen. **No wonder why God created Green leafy vegetables to help keep our blood clean**.

I remember the day my Dad decided that we would start raising cattle. I was so excited to be a cowboy! Nothing is better than waking up at 5:00 am to go bottle feed a calf because the mom had mastitis. I learned a little about cattle; you get a bad strand of cattle you're going to deal with some health problems. Mastitis is one of them. Inflammation in cows? Yep, cows get inflamed too. I remember watching the cows we had in our pasture, grazing on grass always looked lean compared to the bull I would feed oats and corn. I remember asking my dad why don't we just feed the bull grass or hay like the other cows, and he answered: "To fatten em up son to eat." To fatten them up, yep corn and grains fatten a cow up, and grass fed makes the cow leaner. I believe a cow naturally is designed to eat grass, but you know how science is. Always trying to outsmart the laws of nature. When it comes to eating animals, it is best to eat the ones that eat their natural vegetative diet. If you and I eat corn and go to the restroom following that meal, we more than likely see corn. Why? It's because we don't digest it well. **Anything that you don't digest can cause inflammation** which is swelling. I will talk later about storing our toxins in fat cells. Therefore, we get the beer belly following drinking a bunch of beer. So, **it's better to eat grass fed meat than grain fed**. Plus there are more nutrients in a grass-fed animal. Check out the book by Dr. Williams Davis "Wheat Belly."

We need to take the same approach, look at the commercials for dog food. This product is preservative free, no dyes, no high fructose corn syrup, and real food. Wow! Real food. Do you feed your dog, cat, ferret, pig, horse, bird Chocolate bars, Skittles, Donuts, soda products or Candy? I would hope not, but not many people are that crazy. We don't feed this to our animals because it's not good for them, it can make them sick. **While at the same time we neglect our own health by eating this crazy fake food.**

I have run food sensitivity panels on patients from young children up to our geriatric population, and it's astonishing what these demonstrate. I've seen the self-treated holistic patient taking just as many supplements as the drugs my diabetic patient with high blood pressure, high cholesterol, low testosterone, low thyroid, and adrenal fatigue patient is on. I've found that even some of the supplements they are taking is having a mild to moderate reaction. Just because it's good for everyone else, doesn't necessarily mean it may be what works for your best interest that includes supplements as well. So, **if you are having chronic problems, I advise you to seek your health care provider. Ask him or her about testing you for food allergies and or sensitivities, thoroughly check your blood work, rule out any vitamin and mineral deficiencies**18 to see if this could be the missing link to helping you regain that incredible life you have yet to fulfill. If they say no, it is nonsense go find a better educated one who will. **This is the Elephant in the Room!**

What you put into your mouth is extremely important for your brain to function properly, your digestive system to work more efficiently, your skin complexion, the amount of energy and focus you have daily, including your joint and muscle health. Our bodies need proper nutrition to function; we are no super hero and will never break the laws of nature. When you slowly start to use your brain such as thinking more, setting goals and objectives for your day and life, nourishing your immune system with nutrient rich foods. You should consider taking something like whole food nutrition like **Juice PLUS+.** It is whole food fruits, and vegetables slurred up into a glass of juice then dried into a concentrated powder and put into a capsule or gummy for your kids and family to consume. I feed my little girl the gummies, and she is 15 months old.

I believe with consistent, healthy and mental choices you will regain your life and your health back!

Best rule I would give is with Diet:

1. Shop on the outside aisles when in grocery store

2. Eat foods that God created such as fruits and vegetables, organic when possible

3. Drink plenty of clean water, alkaline occasionally

4. Read and research food labels, don't take someone word for it.

5. Pray and be grateful for what you have and that what you eat will nourish your body

6. Eat grass fed, free range and organic meat when possible

7. Try to eliminate gluten, dairy, and soy foods (even organic)

8. Consider taking a quality probiotic

9. Reduce sugar intake (stay away from high fructose corn syrup, saccharin, aspartame)

10. Avoid condiments in plastic bottles (acidity can absorb the plastic)

At the end of the book is a basic 7 day diet, that may help benefit you.

.

CHAPTER 3:

Inflammation

We have all heard about inflammation, that it may be the source of our aches and pains, rashes, brain fog, chronic fatigue, digestive disorders, and even clogged arteries. Do yourself a favor and look up inflammation and chronic health disorders and diseases. Wow! So much information on Google is confirming that inflammation leads to chronic diseases. What can you do with this kind of information? You now find out what in the world that you are doing a daily basis that could be contributing to your inflammation. **Could it be your tooth paste, or bathing soap, your perfume, the Styrofoam cup you pour your coffee in, the flame retardant in your carpet or comforter, the mold in your apartment closet, the genetically modified food, the Gluten or Dairy that is added to your artificial foods?** I believe this is a great place to start. **Think about what you encounter daily from the time you wake up to the time you go to bed, what you feed yourself, what you put on your skin, what you breathe, etc**. Write it down, start taking notes of what's going on. Keep this log for 21 days and document if you have any symptoms, even document the positives like a little more energy, more sleep, and even less pain.

Let's figure out what our triggers are then we are going to try and remove them. Get them out of your daily regimen or routine. We are going to start by knowing what we encounter daily, then make sure we improve our daily routines and dietary choices. **I challenge you to eat more fresh fruits and vegetables, drink more water, and walk that extra quarter mile.**

If money isn't too tight, I would even try a good quality fish oil and even some turmeric with black pepper extract in it. These two are common natural anti-inflammatories that I use in my private practice that I have seen work great. Other additional products work such as Glucosamine Chondroitin, Magnesium, Boswellia, and resveratrol.

I want to move to a topic that we can all relate to. Imagine that coworker, who comes to work every morning, seems like she's short of breath, she woke up this morning saying she hit the snooze 4-5x times before crawling out of bed, she drank her coffee, stopped at the gas station to pick up an energy drink and diet coke, with a candy bar and even a pack of cigarettes. She comes to work, her hair is starting to thin out, she has yellow nails, her skin looks dehydrated, and she gripes every time you ask her to come to your desk for help because of her plantar fasciitis or bilateral knee pain. I am not here to poke fun; I am giving you a reality check if you are ready for it.

This woman typically would suffer from eventually Diabetes, Low Thyroid, Irritable Bowel, Fibromyalgia and possibly even an autoimmune disease if she went to an up to date Rheumatologist. Would you reckon that she has a lot of inflammation going on (stress in her body)? Do you think she is on tackle box full of pharmaceuticals? If not, she's on track to have a handful. Imagine if she knew that what she is putting into her body has a significant impact on her health. **Those pills go to the same place our food does.** Every day she is slowly digging her own grave without knowing what she is doing to herself. It is my opinion that if people truly knew that what they eat has such a significant impact on their health, they would slow it down and make some changes. But, then there are the people that smoke a pack cigarettes a day and know that it causes lung cancer or COPD, but they continue to smoke.

Let me give you an example of drinking a diet soda that I frequently give to my patients daily: When you put something difficult to break down in your body, it goes into your stomach and send this alarm off. Havoc! We got a foreign substance in our body; we need to get rid of this thing before it starts causing damage. So, your immune system gets upregulated and tells your body to get ready for battle. Imagine this alarm system going off all day long, simply because you are not eating and nourishing your body as you should have. Eventually, your body starts to break down; things don't work as well as they used to, you don't overcome your common illnesses like you used to or even slowly start to gain more weight. What in the world is going on? If you are ready for it, then here are your answer: If your body can no longer detoxify or get rid of toxins, you will start to accumulate toxins and inflammation in your fat cells. This process of taking these toxins and by products and storing them in your fat cells requires quite a bit of energy. Then the more toxins and by products we can't get rid of, we will slowly see the weight we put on. If you want to see how toxic you are, see if your doctor or health care provider will check you for any heavy metals? Heavy metals in my body? Oh, that's just the beginning.

Wake up and smell the coffee! If you drink coffee in the morning like me, then you may want to take off the plastic lid[1], so the acidity from the coffee doesn't pull any plastic from your lid. Just trying to inform you on some of the little things that can eventually make a big difference. Did you know coffee; it may even protect you from getting Parkinson's disease per a research article[2]? Did you know that Parkinson's patients have a lack of sense of smell[3], they have issues smelling the coffee, peppermint, and anise[4]? They even have a test for Alzheimer's awareness called the Peanut Butter Test[5]. Check it out! While we are on the topic of inflammation, I wanted to mention that research has even come out that one of the first signs of neurodegeneration is lack of smell and or diminished smell, and constipation[6]. Could our intestines have any impact on our brain? You bet! Imagine if you have inflammation in your digestive system, you don't think it could hinder the brain function such as ADHD, hyperactivity, brain fog, dizziness, and migraines.

I have a theory on arthritis and even disc degeneration. You have this individual, with some comorbidity such as a hypoactive thyroid, adrenal fatigue, and maybe some gastrointestinal dysfunction. They are unaware of how powerful diet and lifestyle is, so they eat the typical American diet. Inflammation is perpetuation daily for months, possibly years. The bones that are in our bodies are white, loaded with calcium. The body is self-healing and will break itself down to help survive. Calcium is used in the body as a buffering system when it tries to balance our ph. or acidity. Think about that phosphoric acid drink, your body can possibly break itself down such as extracting calcium from the bones to help balance out the inflammation or acidity in the blood. This system could repeatedly perform this mechanism daily in small scales reducing our bone density leading to osteoarthritis, osteopenia, degenerative joint disease, and spontaneous fractures. It's just a thought!

CHAPTER 4:

Genes vs. Jeans

I decided after I finished writing this book, to include this chapter. Please do not take any offense to this but it's something that needs to be said. Having a practice in Southwest Louisiana were the fried food, steak rice and gravy, beer drinking, and good times. We have a population of very obese people, heart disease, diabetes, strokes, cardiovascular disorders, and digestive disorders that are a byproduct of our Southern Diet. I have performed thousands of exams, and my patients tell me that they have High Blood Pressure, Diabetes, and Digestive disorders because it's in their genes. I think it's because of the size jeans they wear.

I do not say that in a disrespectful way, I say this in a truthful way. Our bones were not designed to carry all this extra weight; we eat in excess which creates weight gain and bigger jeans. The bigger the jeans, the more health problems and more prone we are to having a genetic disorder or malfunction. So, if you eat fried chicken 4-5x a week and have cardiovascular disease or diabetes, you are self-implementing your chronic disease. It's not because your parents or grandparents made you have a chronic disease, they may have poorly demonstrated proper eating and gave you some weaker genes, but they are not the direct cause of your health problem. Quit making excuses for your health and take ownership. You have the key to opening that door to health or that trip to the hospital.

I am a big fan of epigenetics and genetic testing. Do I believe in genetics?

Absolutely but when it comes to a chronic disease, I believe that we self-inflict our way to most of them. You know that your immune system can turn on and turn off gene expression? Stress applied to genes can also create problems like a mom not taking a good prenatal vitamin when she's pregnant causing her little one to have a neurological defect.

See how important nutrition is, it can even affect our genes as well as our jeans. If you are gaining weight, look at what you are eating, go see your healthcare provider to rule out any food allergies or sensitivities, get your thyroid checked out, check for TPO antibodies, and check your liver markers out. Don't just wait around and let it get out of control; you don't need a bigger sized wardrobe. You need to figure out what the heck is going on; your heart must work harder for every extra pound of fat you add on.

Save your wallet, your joints, your brain, genes, jeans and save your immune system.

CHAPTER 5:

Stimulation

This is my favorite information in the book, and I hope you take notes. The brain is one of the most intricate systems in our bodies. Our brain controls everything from our immune system, organs, pain, muscle strength, and coordination, to our reality.

One of my professors, Dr. Robert Mellilo, author of the most impressive books on Autism and ADHD "Disconnected Kids" writes that the brain requires two specific functions to develop properly.

1. Fuel in the form of oxygen and glucose

2. Stimulation; a healthy sensory system is essential to healthy brain development because it is the solo driver of stimulation to the brain.

He also has taught that the primary vestibular area in the brain that processes vestibular information resides on the right side of the brain and lies very close to the part of the brain that controls the digestive system and the sense of taste or smell, the right frontal insular cortex. The vestibular system is an important system that the brain uses to help with our equilibrium, regulating muscle tone and posture, and assisting in calibration. The insular cortex is a very popular area in the brain that may be underdeveloped in kids with sensory disorders such as Autism or Functional Disconnection Syndrome1.

If you were like me, had a couple of too many drinks before you may notice that your balance could be slightly altered after a few shots of Vodka. I would like to give you a demonstration of what goes on. You drink this alcohol, and your body should metabolize and hopefully detoxify it. Let's use our average college student, who doesn't take any nutritional support and lives off ramen noodles and ham sandwiches. The liver in this individual is more than likely stressed out, due to lack of nutrients and excessive amounts of alcohol. Unable to metabolize the alcohol and detoxify it out of the body, the vestibular system (canals in your ear) get affected due to the inflammation. These canals assist in your balance and coordination along with your posture. No wonder why Jimmy can't walk when he drinks an 18 pack of beer or Sally gets nauseated and dizzy the next day or drinking. Billy can't get off the toilet the next day after a long night of the 10 or 12-ounce curls.

Even alcohol can cause inflammation, which presents its self as a neurological dysfunction. People get dizzy, can't talk, and even pass out with excessive amounts. A connection must soon be made that maybe what touches our stomach or intestines can have an impact on our brain.

Dr. Mellilo also mentions in his book that the brain is the controller of the immune response. The immune system is a great example of how the two hemispheres of the brain work together as a whole. The immune system resides in both sides of the brain, but each hemisphere has its distinct jobs. The left side of the brain acts as the National Guard; it activates antibodies when illness threat. The right side of the brain suppresses the immune system by prevenient it from becoming overactive1. What if you could get both sides of the brain to communicate better by properly stimulating it and feeding it every day. That's what we are about to teach you.

Our brain requires a healthy sensory system to maintain brain development by what we exposure it with: sight, smell, touch, taste, and even hear. These sensory inputs can help the brain develop, get stronger, function and focus better, and have better control. We will break each one of these down into a form of therapy for daily intervention that you can use at home.

CHAPTER 6:

Sound

I am from southern Louisiana, and music is a big part of our culture. We have festivals down here that have great music to dance and listen to. We also have some Casinos here that always bring a few good bands every year that my wife and I will listen to. Music is powerful in that it can help with your studying, coping with a breakup or losing a loved one, and maybe even helping optimize your rehab program following a stroke[1,2,3,4]. Music is therapeutic, but it's also a great sensory input to the brain.

My grandmother would always tell me that classical music was going to make me smarter if I would listen to it. As a child, it was like pulling teeth for me to listen to it. But now, after I know the benefit of sound and music, I give it a 5-star rating for optimizing brain function. Research has proved that music causes global activation of the brain[5] and may help increase dopamine function in the brain[6,7,8,9]. Even muscles move better with rhythm[10]. We have seen patients come into our office, following a serious stroke and spent countless hours in rehab still unable to ambulate properly and have the function of their affected limb. We vibrate their muscles, get them activated while they listen to some specific targeted rhythmic stimulation and they move. They move better than they ever had sometimes even after just one treatment. Why? When you properly stimulate the brain, it's amazing what kind of outcome you will get. Do you use music as a part of your daily sensory stimulation?

I get asked all the time, what kind of music do you listen to? Well, I listen to a little bit of everything: I like country, I love worship music, and I enjoy house and classical music. What about the others? Well, it's just not my taste, but I do advise you listen to something that doesn't promote hate, drugs, violence, and destruction. What you feed the brain whether it's from the news or even your music helps assist in the function of your brain.

What about the news? Well, I can tell you that I would rather read the news that listens to it. I grew up with the news on the television screen; talk about some depressing information on the news. I mean, you get 60 minutes of just gloom, the world's going to end, they sky has strange white lines, an earthquake just occurred, the honey bees are dying, genetically modified food isn't as bad as the people on social media say it (yea right!), or the cure for cancer is just around the corner (is it really? This stuff has been in the news since the 60s) Wake up! What can you do besides just get full of fear listening to this stuff? How about you just change the channel to something more positive like sports or travel or do like I do, cut it off. Don't feed your mind with all this negativity because what you hear can make an impact on your health. Think about how much money is spent on commercials during the Super Bowl? I don't think they just those companies freely throw money out the door if it wasn't effective.

If you don't believe me, then give me a roundabout on how many drug commercials do you see in 30-minute television show or series, or even on the radio? Man, it's depressing but the worse is having to listen to all the side effects and then at the end may even cause death. What? Death, geez I'm just trying to watch Shark week, and this drug is telling me if I take it I will feel like I am in a field of daisy's running after the sunset, but it may cause death or worse symptoms than just my depression. I'm better off reading a book or listening to paid free advertisement radio.

I am a proud parent of a beautiful little princess. I love my daughter; she looks just like her mother thankfully. When my wife found out she was pregnant, I started playing music to her belly. Music is powerful, I would play Baby Mozart on Pandora, Washed by the Water by Need to Breathe, Jack Johnson, John Mayer, and Sam Hunt. A little diversity but sound is therapeutic. I would drive my wife insane talking and play music to my little future trophy. The day she was born, I can remember us in the delivery room jamming out to Worship music. God is about to give us the best gift in the world, and we are going to jam out to music honoring him. Men, if your wife has your child, you know that feeling of respect you have for them after they just went to battle. Women are heroes; there is no way a man could have a baby. I don't care how macho he is. Back to my story, so my daughter is born, and the nurse takes her for her first bath. I go grab my Bluetooth speaker, bring it over next to my daughter, and play the song that I repeatedly played for 9 months "Washed by the Water." The nurse warned me beforehand that she may scream loud during the bath, but it was perfectly normal, not my little princess. She was the calmest baby enjoying her first bath to an incredible song. Music is calming; music is therapeutic, music is extremely powerful if used in the right way.

Every day, when I get home from work, we turn on the music. We dance just about every night of the week. Who doesn't like good music? Turn that television off, put your phone down. Sit on the back porch, turn on Pandora, Amazon Radio or fire up the radio and relax.

CHAPTER 7:

Sight

Vision is necessary just like light is important to us as well. Most of us have smart phones and computer screens, high definition television, and occasionally virtual reality headsets. What if the lights on the screens or the over use of them may contribute to our insomnia, migraines, and even attention1? I have watched a countless number of patients on sleep medication and aids, tell me that they work in front of computers all week then spend all weekend laid up on the couch watching Netflix or playing video games. What's wrong with this picture? You're not out there getting sunlight, getting your muscles activated, strengthen your weight bearing joints, and sweating the toxins out your body. People sit there, sedentary watching a computer monitor. Natural light can be beneficial for you if you have sleep disturbances, someone's waking up early and watching the sunrise and sun set while taking a walk2 may be just what you need to do for a week or so. I bet you will find this to become very therapeutic. I have watched kids with hyperactivity or attention deficit issues, improve their focus by using eye movement exercises3 such as gaze fixation exercises and placing the book or notepad in the upper left or upper right corner of the table to desk. Movement is the key, even with your eyes.

One day, I had a new patient that was diagnosed with Insomnia. I always read my charts before I walk into the exam room, so I have an idea of what's going on. This individual wrote he had insomnia for 7 years. I can't even imagine what it's like to go 2-3 days of no sleep, like my old college days cramming for finals. After finals, I could have crawled into a dark hole and slept for weeks. Sleep deprivation will harm your brain, especially your memory and social skills. Anyways, this individual was on the typical sleep deprived Cocktail pharmaceuticals. Depended on the drug to sleep, not bad for business! I've read enough business books that seems like the best business is not sales, it's called the reorder business. Don't fix the problem, make it easier to cope with so you keep them coming back for more. So, I ask this patient about his diet and how much exercise he gets. He laughs at me like I'm crazy. Exercise, yeah right! How can I exercise when I have no energy?

I will never forget this day, so I decide to tell him the answer that no one wants to be told. You need to clean your diet up, start taking some vitamins and minerals, and you need to watch some sunrises and sunsets. I get another laugh; he tells me I'm crazy. You think that if I eat better, start exercising and watch the sunrise and sunset every day that I will start to sleep better? That's like asking me I know the alphabet. It's common sense, that's something everyone no matter who you are or what condition you have should do. That's how simple life is, eat what's put here naturally for you to eat and enjoy the beginning and end of the day. Two weeks later, my patient shows up, and I walk into the room, and he's laughing, he then precedes to tell me that he has been sleeping like a baby angel since he took my advice. He told me that he had put night shades on his house 7 years ago, he wanted to darken his house so that he could sleep better. After he realized how important natural light and good nutrition is, he could successfully get off his meds after talking with his Medical Doctor. Did I work magic? Sometimes I think I do, but I just go back to the basics with every problem. Most of the time, it's the small things that are the answer to our problem.

I work with Parkinson's patients, and I notice that they have slow eye movements4 when I ask them to follow my penlight or finger when I make an H in space. I notice kids with ADHD have slight abnormal eye movements[5] when ask to track or have the inability to focus on a dot for longer than 5 seconds. This is a problem; this is a dysfunction that needs to be corrected. We are in the pill phase where we take a pill for everything, but how about we start to locate and define our weakness and start to improve the small things. Every journey begins with a small step forward. Let's notice how beautiful nature is, watch birds fly throughout the sky, watch leaves blow in the wind, go for a nice drive in the country or walk the streets in your town looking at the tops of buildings. Enjoy nature! Enjoy natural light. This can help you out.

I went to private school when I was a child, one of the things I can still remember about my fourth-grade teacher Mrs. Chamblee was Kyle keep your eyes on your paper. It makes me laugh, every time I think of this because if I didn't know the answer, I wanted to know where it was? Was it on the paper of the kid next to me or the paper of the smart girl to the front right of me? I bring this up, because if you are trying to recall some elapsed answer to the question, what do you do with your eyes? Most people look up, when you look up with your eyes, it fires into a part of the brainstem called the midbrain[6,7] (this is where the neurotransmitter dopamine is produced). Imagine if you could consistently tap into this area by doing a series of vertical eye movements?

Have you ever been on a vacation where you may have been to a beach, the mountains, or even the Grand Canyon? Have you noticed the beauty in this scenery? How did it make you feel? Can you remember? More than likely, it may have had a therapeutic benefit such as releasing some endorphins (your feel-good neurochemistry messengers'). Imagine if we could capture these movements and feel like this all the time? With advancements in technology, we will soon see the benefits of cyber therapy or the powerful impacts virtual reality has on neurological and psychiatric problems. There is research that demonstrates the impact on visual stimulation and melatonin[8], or visual stimulation and dopamine[9] (neurotransmitters that help you focus, even serotonin [neurotransmitters that help with mood]).

Could they be the future therapeutic intervention for ADHD, PTSD, and even chronic pain disorders?

CHAPTER 8:

Touch

Have you ever noticed that a newborn baby loves to be held, rocked, and bundled up? The stimulation helps the brain develop. I have worked with numerous kids that have been adopted by some incredible parents, they adopt these children with sensory disorders. They were deprived of love, physical touch while their parents were out drinking, partying, and Facebooking. If you have a young born child, hold them, play with them, talk with them, their environment helps to build their brain.

We resist gravity by using our large muscles and joints1. When rats used their muscles and joints in new and interesting ways, they showed increased plasticity and growth within their brain2. Decreased muscle tone is directly related to a decrease in stimulation to the brain, especially the higher learning and thinking3. This is some useful knowledge, so if you don't use it, you lose it kind of stuff. Think about how many people struggle to get 5,000 steps in. We are seeing a whole market of digital health tracking devices that are trying to inform us that we don't walk enough, we don't use our cardiovascular system to exercise. We set goals just to make 10,000 steps daily. We need to be moving as much as we can! Life is all about motion if you aren't moving around enjoying the life you are patiently degenerating on your couch.

Do you know that some of my ADD/ADHD kids can't even do a jumping jack, snap their fingers, catch a ball, and even squat without falling? What in the world is wrong with this? Take a nice stroll through a crowded subdivision, and I can tell you what you won't see? You won't see kids running around playing basketball or jumping roping; they are inside playing on their smart phone or glued to their gaming devices. If you have kids, and this sounds like your kids then you need to get them involved in some form of exercise: swimming, soccer, baseball, softball, fishing, cycling, volleyball, golf, cheer, dance, you name it. Get them out the house and get them active.

Every day I see a child who is overweight, it just makes me cringe up. Why start now at this age with overweight and toxic? This kid will eventually have health problems down the road that could be prevented right now, making him eat better, signing him up for recreational sports, get him moving and feed this kid right. Don't get him chicken nuggets, French fries, carbonated drinks, mac n cheese, ice cream, and carbonated drinks. Get this child some nutrients, feed him something that will give him energy and make him stay healthy.

What kind of exercises should I do? We start with jump roping, jumping jacks, cross crawl exercises, balancing on a Bosu ball, using resistance bands to perform Y, T, and A's, rows, lat pull downs, knee extension, kickbacks, medicine ball rotations, gaze fixation exercises, elliptical, stationary bicycle, and yoga poses.

We even make patient perform vagal nerve exercises[4] such as gargling water in the morning after they brush their teeth, trying to see if they can make their eyes tear up or laying on their back trying to perform diaphoretic breathing exercises[5]. Even singing is a great way to improve your brain. Playing musical instrument such as the piano, guitar, drums, saxophone, bass, etc.

Stimulate the brain, did you know that movement even activates BDNF[4] (brain derived neurotrophic factor). Brain Derived Neurotrophic factor prevents the death of existing brain cells and supports in cognitive function. So, get out and move, do coordinated exercises such as draw the alphabet with your left pinky or make figure 8s with your right leg.

Consider the acupressure system. We have utilized that ancient alternative therapy practice that has been around since the Bible. Is this a hoax? The acupressure system proves that our brain and bodies work like a computer and a keyboard. You select the right button or type in a specific code, out comes some fascinating results such as reduction in pain, fewer migraine headaches, problems with infertility and bladder dysfunctions, to bolstering the immune system. We have used low powered lasers, Muscle or Tens pads over points, and even manually rubbed certain points that have worked with our patients.

If you have a child with sensory disorders, he or she may benefit with trying to stimulate the right side of the brain more by activating the left side of the body. We do a lot of sensory stimulation in our office on the left side of the body for example: vibrating the left arm and leg, making figure 8's with the left arm and leg, doing piano fingers with the left arm while balancing on a Bosu ball, exercises on the elliptical while they are focusing on a dot in the upper left visual field. Small things like that over time can contribute to a better healthier brain if you start feeding it the right nutrients as well. Both proper sensory stimulation and nutrition can be very therapeutic. Gluten Free and Dairy free diets can make a big difference. Check these children for Mineral and Vitamin deficiencies, stool samples, food sensitivities, anemia, digestive dysfunctions. If they were a C-section baby, check their probiotic status. Find out why they still have Primitive reflexes? Locate weakness and correct them.

My wife and I were going to church one Sunday, as we were walking up, I saw this homeless man sitting outside the church. He obviously looked nervous to go into the doors. The closer we got to the man, one of our church members walked up to the guy, sat down, shook his hand then gave this man a huge hug. It made me smile! You know that was just what that man may have needed, just someone to care, someone just to lay their hand on him.

This paragraph is for the athlete or weekend warrior. Purchase a hand-held vibration massager or Sports massager off Amazon. Vibrate your muscles, look at each muscle when you vibrate it. Make the brain more aware of where it is in space. I have worked with NFL wide receivers, and most of their therapy is them standing on a Vibe Plate Platform, listening to targeted sounds, while they are watching either a computer monitor performing reaction time, peripheral vision exercises, or playing interactive balance games balancing on a Bosu ball. That's a lot of sensory input, but I'm trying to activate a lot of different muscles.

I love Vibration therapy! Vibration can help with your balance and coordination, activate muscles, increase blood flow, and reduce edema or swelling in joints. You have poor balance, vibrate your big muscles such as your quads, qlutes, spinal muscles, IT band, posterior deltoid. Get the postural muscles activated, increase blood flow to all your extensor muscles, stimulate that brain.

CHAPTER 9:

Pain

Pain and suffering are things that I do not wish upon anyone. Pain can eventually lead to insomnia, divorce, addictions, and bankruptcy. I believe everyone encounters some form of pain in their life. Nearly 92 million U.S. adults, or about 38 percent of the population, took a legitimately prescribed opioid like OxyContin or Percocet in 2015, per results from the National Survey on Drug Use and health. That is more than 1 in 3 Americans prescribed opioids in 2015.

Did you know that pain is experienced in the brain, it's not experienced in the joint, muscle, bone, or organ? Think about the Diabetic family member that had a limb amputated due to poor circulation and an infection in their foot. Even after 5 years, they still think their toe itches when it has been surgically removed. It's because the brain has a map (somatotopic) of the entire body, it sends signals to get feedback from all areas of your body. When the limb is removed, the geographical location in the brain is still there, checking how that toe and foot are doing. It's not there anymore, so then the brain questions send out a stress signal, and pain can be experienced. Without a limb, pain is experienced.

I have countless patients that have tried just about every round of pain pills, injections, nerve blocks, and even surgical intervention still having pain. Once you run out of options as a Doctor, you then play the blame game and tell patients it's their fault or it's in their head. It works for most people, but I guess it's not going to work for you. So, then you get depressed, your anxiety goes up, having a hard time sleeping, then it starts to spike your blood pressure. Whoa, that's at least 3-4 new drugs you just got added to your regimen. That's enough to give your doctor carpel tunnel writing prescriptions all day long. You may feel as if no one can help you anymore, you have tried it all. You may think you have until you find out about a functional neurologist, an out the box Physical Therapy, or an incredible chiropractor.

Sometimes surgical procedures are necessary, but some could have been prevented if you seek proper treatment. What blows my mind is when someone has a muscle ache or knee problem, and their first trip is to their family medicine practitioner. They are prescribed a muscle relaxer, anti-inflammatory, or pain meds then go home and get constipated within a few days. The prescription runs out, and the pain is still there, well your liver just took a nice pounding while the problem persists. Go see a Chiropractor, Physical therapist, Orthopedic doctor, or even a massage therapist. Go see someone that can teach you how to properly rehab a muscle, instead of just taking a pill for every ache. Take an example of a cell phone tower, it's this incredibly build structure with a frame and anchored down with wires and cables. This tower can sustain some force and weather. If the structure or frame gets some damage, you think they climb up and slap some super glue on it? No, because then the next storm or heavy wind would do more damage. It's a similar analogy I use in my private practice, I call it the band aid approach. Instead of looking at the problem, assessing whether there is an anchor problem, a frame problem, a nutrient problem, a circulation or balance problem, we just band aid with a pill or an injection. To give you an example of our therapy. We have you fill a long list of intake questions out, then ask you if you are open to suggestion on nutrition. Our patient's that select the nutrition, are then given another sheet to check off specific conditions such as stomach pains, eczema, blood sugar, muscle spasms, and migraines. We then perform an orthopedic and neurological exam testing to see if you have any muscle injuries or weakness and assessing your balance/coordination and nerve function. It's very seldom that we see someone who is in perfect condition. I've tested Olympic athletes and still find muscle imbalances, center of gravity alterations, diminished eye movements, and inability to focus.

We then proceed to treat you after we determine a treatment plan suited for your recovery. This treatment regimen is very effective: Virtual Reality, Low Powered Laser, Vestibular rehab, Vibration therapy, Neurosage, Therapeutic Exercises, Gait Training, Applied Kinesiology, Ultrasound and Interferential, Music therapy, Essential Oils, Holographic patches, Manual Therapy, and Chiropractic (manual and instrumentation).

That's quite a regimen, I have watched someone with frozen shoulder (unable to lift their arm 90 degrees) after spending 6 months in Therapy come in and one session regain full function of their shoulder. With the lack of understanding the brain, it may seem reasonable to think this is impossible. However, if you understand how to properly stimulate the brain by firing into it properly with targeted sensory input, then this is a no brainer. I will give you just a little hint of how we do this, we use eye movements while the patient is listening to specific rhythmic sounds, vibrating the affected area while lasering or stim over an acupressure point.

Do not be the patient that wakes up first thing in the morning saying "I wonder what joint or what part of my body is going to hurt today." I am a stickler for attaching anything negative to I AM, Can't, Wont, and Failure. Every day you have a choice to be Positive or Negative, to do good or do bad, to be happy or sad, to enjoy life or be depressed. The choice is ours, use your mind to your advantage. Be careful what you wish or declare!

You may have got diagnosed with an autoimmune disease or cancer. If so, are you just going to sit around and wait for someone else to help you or you going to figure out how to beat this challenge? The Bible states in Isiah 41:10 "Do not fear for I am with you, do not be afraid for I am your God, I will strengthen you, I will help you." Pray that God will lead you to the best

Open Minded Doctors, pray that you will eat the most nutritious meals that are helping you to regain your health, and thank God that he is healing you. Don't doubt one bit, understand that regaining your health is a journey, it's may be some ups and downs, but keep on regaining your health, don't stop. Keep going, Thank Jesus Christ for healing you. Don't let your poor diets or negative thinking hinder you from regaining your life back!

CHAPTER 10:

What can I do about it?

So now you know. I believe that I have provided you with enough information to jump start your health no matter how young or old you are.

I am a big fan of research and education; I think that you need to take it upon yourself and do your own homework. Watch the documentaries such as Food Matters and Hungry for a change. Read Dr. Junger Book "Clean Gut" or Datis Kharzzian: "Why isn't my brain working." Don't make excuses that you don't have enough time, or that you don't like to read. Break this cycle now, and do it.

Find which diet works best for you whether it's a Gluten and Diary Free, Mediterranean, Paleo, Specific Carbohydrate Diet, Fodmap, or Clean Gut 21-day protocol. I have found that one of these will work great in most of my patient's recovery. At the end of the book, you will see a basic 7-day diet that I put most of my patients on.

Find a healthcare practitioner that is open minded, find one that is on the cutting edge of treatment interventions, if you see the one that practices like a dinosaur, you may not get the results you desire. You must make a change to get a change. So, change it up, go see an alternative practitioner if you haven't, go see a functional medicine doctor, talk with your Medical Doctor about testing you for Vitamin and Mineral Deficiencies. Find the root of the problem and don't settle for an average treatment.

I challenge you to write down the person you want to become, write down the experiences that you will have, and what kind of contribution will you make once you obtain this ideal person or even. Let me give you an example. I had a patient who was diagnosed with Multiple Sclerosis, she went thru the regular treatments: meds, anti-inflammatories, nerve blocks, steroid shots, and even plasma transfusions. When she came to see me, she was dizzy, holding on to the wall when she would walk down the hall, and in excruciating pain. I asked her to give me a goal of something she wanted to achieve, and it was these 2 things:

1. To no longer be dizzy

2. For my MS to go into remission

So, we took these goals, and the next was, for me to achieve these goals, what do I have to do? Her answers were

- To eat better

- To avoid gluten, dairy, processed foods, sugar, and alcohol

- To take my medication and vitamins

- To exercise

- To have no fear

I was excited because now we were given the brain and immune system some ammo. The last question was once you overcome this obstacle what will you do, what kind of contribution will you make?

- To teach people that if I can overcome this illness, then anyone can

- To help support other people out there suffering from the same condition

Below is a sample of how I personally and in my practice help patients with overcoming obstacles. I have achieved some incredible goals with this formula.

"Every well built house started in the form of a definite purpose plus a definitive plan in the nature of a set of blueprints" Napoleon Hill

This is my formula/ blueprint I use daily
1. Read it first thing in the morning after saying your prayers and thanking God for what he has blessed you with
2. Read it at the end of the day right before bed.
3. If you get depressed, sad, knocked down, stepped on, laughed at, read your blue print

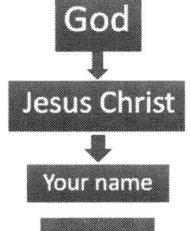

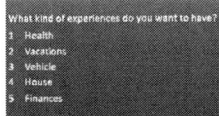 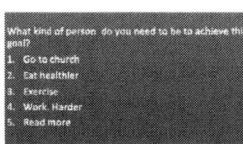 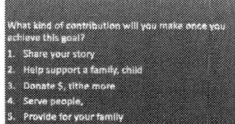

A little knee time is something I recommend. Get on your knees, thank God, be grateful for your life. Pray that God is healing you, pray that your immune system is gaining strength, pray that God is guiding you to achieve your goal.

CHAPTER 11:

Mental Fitness

We see a rise in neurological disorders such as dementia, Parkinsons, ADHD, Depression, Traumatic Brain Injuries and bipolar that are frequently treated with pharmaceuticals. **Our primary answer for addressing those fundamental disorders has been the chemical drink or cocktail designed to rebalance or correct or attenuate already-distorted brain chemistry**[1]. What about going see a Life Coach, someone that can teach you different coping mechanisms to your problems such as exercising, writing down positive goals and affirmations, and even eating better foods. I see people all the time that are depressed. I always ask them why they are depressed. They just tell me they are depressed. I try to dig deeper and then the truth comes out. People simply don't like what they are doing; they are tired of feeling like they are breaking, their marriages are suffering because the bills are stacking up or their children are going off the deep end. But if you continue to go about your daily routine without making any significant change, you are going to wake up tomorrow with the same problems you face today. Face your problems! Face your fears! Face reality, and quit making excuses that you can't exercise because there isn't enough of time or it's too expensive to eat healthily. When you add it up, in the long run, I would rather spend money on better quality food than some pain meds, diabetic medication, or chemotherapy.

Excuses are problems, we all have them. But it's when we realize that we are indecently holding ourselves back from achieving our goals, beating that chronic disease, and even achieving that Greek Sculpture frame. **You must make time; you must cherish your time; you must stay focused.** Time will slip by faster than you know it, so give yourself some goals, set some vacations or trips, save that extra money for helping Sofia in Guatemala get necessities to live a better life.

I enjoy watching success whether it's in health, sports, business and even spiritual! It's incredible to watch people find their purpose, their dream, their Why? **We should all wake up every morning, grateful but with a purpose. If we have a purpose and a direction, we shall never perish.** One of my favorite verses: Proverbs 4: 25-26 "Look straight ahead and fix your eyes on what lies before you. Mark out a straight path for our feet. Stay on the safe path." Mathew 21:21 "I tell you the truth, if you have faith and don't doubt, you can do things like this and much more. You can even to say to this mountain, may you be lifted up and thrown into the seas and it will happen." **Write down your goal, declare your goal, and know that God will help you achieve it if you don't doubt or have fear**!

Personal development books fill the book shelves in my library at home. I started reading them following Chiropractic school. Initially, I decided to go out on my own and start my private practice. I was loaded with more health information that I could drive someone crazy with health information, but I did not know how to run a business. One night at a wedding, a mentor of mine walked up to me and asked me how things were going. I tried to pretend like things were going good, and he could read past me as he is a current business man. He told me that if I would do these two things life would get better:

1. Get to church tomorrow

2. Read the Law of Success by Napoleon Hill.

I decided to wake up and go to church, and this was the day my life changed! Changed, exploded, potential, awareness, and faith were discovered. The worship music during the service I went to moved me as I had never been moved before. I knew at that moment, my goal, my life, my purpose was to get all this information I stored in my head out to the world. I then purchased "Laws of Success" by Napoleon Hill and started reading at 11:15 am. I read this book all night long into the next few days. I didn't put it down, but I took notes. I have an entire notebook from what I learned. So, then I decided to put my knowledge into practice. I wrote my goal, my destination, my dreams that I would one day become an International Speaker about the Brain and Rehabilitation, my practice would attract people from all over the world, and I would start a computer company that would change the rehabilitation world. I have achieved these goals!

I mentioned that I attended private school, well I was an extremely gifted kid when it came to athletics. Maybe to my bias, but I had some impressive fine motor and coordination skills. What I did lack was the comprehension of stories, the lack of the big picture, the being calm without fidgeting, and lack of attention skills. I was diagnosed with ADHD, allergies, colic, reflux, speech impediment, and even pigeon toed. I had to go to speech therapy, wear shoes on the opposite foot, go to the allergist to get my painful shots, and the pediatrician to get antibiotic for my inner ear infections. My parents did a phenomenal job of raising me, and I give them so much credit to that person I am today. My parents both hard working people, with a little money and always made sure we were involved in church, sports, and academics. My mom would take me to speech therapy, and I can still remember the therapist trying to get me to say "R's." It was so frustrating for me because I would say Wabbit and Wed instead of Rabbit and Red. I would hear kids make fun of me because I couldn't talk right, or people commenting on my crooked feet. As a child, I can remember thinking I'm going to show these people; I'm going to one day talk normal and walk normally. You know I was the starting quarterback for my high school 5A football team, started shortstop and even went to play Collegiate

Baseball. **Here is this kid with a physical disability, overcomes it and now I am here today to help people make the same recovery.**

I lost a few friends over the duration of this development over the years. But what I gained was a reality that I had only dreamt of. I'm living it; it's here! I wake up to being so grateful for my family, my health, my patients, my business, and my home. I started years ago with a notepad and today still have a notepad. I wake up early in the morning, go for a run and circuit workout, read and write down my short term and long term goals, thank God for what I have and go to the best job in the world. I get to watch people regain their lives back, and there is nothing better than to help someone out. I am fortunate to do this daily, and I am thankful that I get to share this message with you.

1. Set goals, affirmations, and set them Big! Don't cheat yourself

2. Be grateful for everything you have, if your heart is beating you have a purpose and you should be grateful

3. Be prepared for rejections and setbacks

4. When you get knocked down, get back up or as Jesus said to turn the other cheek

5. Try to do something good for someone else today

6. Eat healthy foods such as fruits and vegetables

7. Move, exercises, read, laugh, enjoy good music

8. Be open minded to new suggestions. The greatest poison in life is regret.

9. Know that we all have the DNA of God inside of us, so we do possess Greatness

10. Love people, cherish the small things and live in the moment

I hope this book has positively moved you as this was my intention. I ask that if this book has moved you or if you may have gained any valuable insight from this book, share this with your family and friends. **God, bless you and your family**!

"A mind that is stretched by a new experience can never go back to its old dimensions." Oliver Wendell Holmes

THE PROCESS BEHIND DR. DAIGLE SOFTWARE:

In short, Systemic Neural Adaptation is a noninvasive method and system for creating rapid and sustained neurochemical activation. The process of Systemic Neural Adaptation involves the intentional change over time of bodily systems to **carefully modulated and applied visual, auditory, and physical stimulus**. This systemic change through neural response is achieved through noninvasive non-pharmacologic means enabling the brain and body to work in harmony.

For more information visit us at www.snabiotech.com

Recommended books:

To Regain Health:
1. Clean Gut by Dr. Alejandro Junger

2. Why isn't my brain working? By Datis Kharzzian

3. Eat Right for Your Type by Dr. D'Adamo

Personal Development:

1. Law of Success by Napoleon Hill

2. The Greatest Secret by Earl Nightingale

3. The Power of Subconscious Mind by Joseph Murphy

4. The Traveler's Gift by Andy Andrews

5. The Purpose Driven Life by Rick Warren

6. How to reach your life goals by Peter J. Daniels

Mental Fitness:

1. Man's Search for Meaning by Viktor E. Frankl

2. You are the Placebo by Joe Dispenza

Bible Verses:

1. Proverbs

2. Mathew 6:24-26

3. Mathew 7:7

4. Mathew 9:29

5. Mathew 21:21-22

6. John 5:14

7. Mark 11:24-25

8. Eph 2:10

9. Isiah 58:7-11

BASIC 7 DAY DIET:

Foods to avoid:

Gluten, Whole grain Wheat, Dairy (milk, cheese, yogurt), beer, bread, pasta, corn, soy, alcohol, pork, cold cuts, hot dogs, canned meat, sausage, junk food, processed food, anything with food dyes, artificial colors, fast food restaurants, sodas, Mechanically separated chicken, beef, pork

Ingredients to avoid:

High Fructose corn syrup, Monosodium Glutamate, Wheat, Soy, Genetically Modified, Wheat sugar, Caramel color, Phosphoric acid, Canola Oil, BHT, Corn syrup, Hydrolyzed Soy Protein, Sodium Nitrite, Paraben.

Consider a diet like this:

Breakfast: Choice of Eggs, Turkey Bacon (nitrate free), Protein Bar (Organic Food bar, Kind Bar, Paleo Bar, Gluten Free Oat), Gluten free oat cereal, Fruit (organic when possible: Blueberries, Strawberries, Grapes, Peach, Pear, Plum, Apple)

Mid-morning snack: Choice of Fruit, Vegetables, Organic food bar, Rx Bar, Paleo Bar, Organic Protein Bar.

Lunch: Mixed Green Salad with choice of meat (organic and grass fed if possible) Chicken, Steak, Fish, Lamb, Veal. Avocado, Broccoli, Carrots, Spinach, Beets, Kale.

Afternoon snack: Fruit (organic when possible: banana, apple, berries, grapes, peach, pear plum) Choice of nuts (almonds, cashews, pecans)

Dinner: Broiled/Baked fish, steamed veggies, Mixed green salad, Baked Chicken, Gluten free pasta and shrimp (avoid if allergic to seafood), Lettuce wraps (chicken, beef, veggies), Grass fed meat

Looking for more information Dr. Daigle provided in the book?

Software company: www.snabiotech.com

Nutritional Information: www.facebook.com/UPdocs

To schedule an appointment: www.uperformance.com

Follow Dr. Daigle on **Instagram**: dr.kyledaigle

on **Facebook**: www.facebook.com/updocs

Dr. Brandon Brock and Datis Kharrazian, thank you for teaching me the big picture!

REFERENCES:

Chapter 2:

1. Smith SM. High fructose corn syrup replaces sugar in processed food. *Environ Nutr*1998; **11:7**–8

2. Beverage consumptions: <u>J Acad Nutr Diet.</u> 2016 Jan;116(1):28-37. doi: 10.1016/j.jand.2015.08.009. Epub 2015 Sep 11.

3. CBS News. Study on Genetically Modified Corn, herbicide and tumors reignites controversy. Retrieved from <u>https://www.cbsnews.com/news/study-on-genetically-modified-corn-herbicide-and-tumors-reignites-controversy/</u>

4. Dr. Axe. Phosphoric Acid: The dangerous Hidden Additive You've Likely Consumed. Retrieved from <u>https://draxe.com/phosphoric-acid/</u>

5. McDowall Jennifer (2006 Oct.) Retrieved from <u>https://www.ebi.ac.uk/interpro/potm/2006_10/Page1.htm</u>

6. Kanarek RB. Artificial food dyes and attention deficit hyperactivity disorder. Nutr Rev. 2011; 69:385–91.

7. Rowe AH, editor. Elimination diets and the patient's allergies; a handbook of allergy. Philadelphia: Lea & Febiger; 1944.

8. Feingold BF. Why your child is hyperactive. New York: Random House; 1975.

9. Spergel JM. Eosinophilic esophagitis in adults and children: evidence for a food allergy component in many patients. Curr Opin Allergy Clin Immunol. 2007 Jun;7(3):274-8. Review.

10. McDonalds Restaurant at 22 USA Hospitals. Retrieved from: https://www.vegan.com/blog/mcdonalds-restaurants-at-22-usa-hospitals/

11. Menino Thomas M, Johnson Paula. (2012 April 2) Health care vs. sick care: Why prevention is essential to payment reform. Retrieved from (https://www.bostonglobe.com/opinion/2012/04/02/health-care-sick-care-why-prevention-essential-payment-reform/i0DfqHPvtq2NhHAqbyhAnK/story.html

12. Lupkin, Sydney. (2014 July 17) Boy Who Got Unapproved Drug Heads Home to VIrgina. Retrieved from http://abcnews.go.com/Health/boy-unapproved-drug-heads-home-virginia/story?id=24599780

13. 2014 September 4. How Chemotherapy Affects the immune System. Retrieved from: http://www.breastcancer.org/tips/immune/cancer/chemo

14. Environmental Working Group. (2005 July 14). A Benchmark Investigation Of Industrial Chemicals, Pollutants And Pesticides In Umbilical Cord Blood.

15. NBC News. (2014 Feb 5). Vitamin C may help cancer treatment Study Finds. Retrieved from: https://www.nbcnews.com/health/cancer/vitamin-c-may-help-cancer-treatment-study-finds-n23066

16. ABC News. (2016 Oct) Using Blue Berries to Fight Cancer. Retrieved from: http://abcnews.go.com/Technology/story?id=119873&page=1

17. Roizment Tracey. (2015 Nov 5). Does Chlorophyll Cleanse the Blood. Retrieved from: http://www.livestrong.com/article/407472-what-is-a-healthy-hemoglobin-level/

18. Children's Hospital & Research Center at Oakland (July/August 2009). *Alternative Therapies in Health & Medicine*, http://www.alternative-therapies.com/resources/web_pdfs/recent/0709_morris.pdf

Chapter 3:

1. Ostrovsky Larry, Ostrovsky Oksana. Dangers Lurking In Your Coffee Lid. Retrievewed from: http://www.bewellbuzz.com/wellness-buzz/dangers-in-coffee-lids/

2. Barclay Laurie. Does Coffee Protect Against Parkinsons Disease. Retrieved from: http://www.webmd.com/parkinsons-disease/news/20000523/caffeine-protect-against-parkinsons-disease#2

3. 10 Early Signs of Parkinson's Disease. Retrieved from: http://www.parkinson.org/understanding-parkinsons/10-early-warning-signs

4. Diagnostic Value of the Impairment of Olfaction in Parkinson's Disease

    Swaantje Casjens, Angelika Eckert, Dirk Woitalla, Gisa Ellrichmann, Michael Turewicz, Christian Stephan, Martin Eisenacher, Caroline May, Helmut E. Meyer, Thomas Brüning, Beate Pesch

    PLoS One. 2013; 8(5): e64735. Published online 2013 May 16. doi: 10.1371/journal.pone.0064735

5. Sauer Alissa (2016 Jan 20). Can't Smell Peanut Butter? Alzheimers May be the Culprit! Retrrieved from: http://www.alzheimers.net/2014-09-19/peanut-butter-test-predicts-alzheimers/

Chapter 4:

1. Marvasti FF, Stafford RS. From "Sick Care" to Health Care: Reengineering Prevention into the U.S. System. *The New England journal of medicine.* 2012;367(10):889-891. doi:10.1056/NEJMp1206230.

Chapter 5:

1. Mellilo, Robert. Disconnected Kids: New York: Penguin Group. 2009

Chapter 6:

1. Altenmuller, E. et al (2009) Neural reorganization underlies improvement in stroke-induced motor dysfuntion by music-supoorted therapy. Ann. N.Y. Academy of Sciences. 1169: 395-405

2. Garu-Sanchez, J. et al (2013) Plasticity in the sensorimotor cortex induced by music-supported therapy in stroke patietns: a TMS study. Frontiers in Human Neuroscience. 7, 494

3. Johansson, B.B. (2012) Multisensory stimulation in stroke rehabilitation. Frontiers in human sciences. 6, 60.

4. Jun, E., Roh, Y.H., & Kim, M.J. (2012). The effect of music-movement therapy on physical and psychological states of stroke patients. Journal of Clinical Nursing. 22.21-23

5. Peretz, I. & Zatorre, RJ. (2005) Brain organization for music processing. Annu Rev Psychol. 56.89-114

6. Menon, V. & Levitin, D.J. The rewards of music listening: response and physiological connectivity of the mesolimbic system. *Neuroimage* **28**, 175–184 (2005)

7. Knutson, B. & Gibbs, S.E. Linking nucelus accumbens dopamine and blood oxygenation. *Psychopharmacology (Berl.)* **191**, 813–822 (2007)

8. Wise, R.A. Dopamine, learning and motivation. *Nat. Rev. Neurosci.* **5**, 483–494 (2004)

9. Zald, D.H. & Zatorre, R.J. On music and reward. in *The Neurobiology of Sensation and Reward* (ed. Gottfried, J.A.) (CRC Press, 2011)

10. Safranek, M.G., Koshland, G.F., & Raymond, G. (1982) Effect of auditory rhythm on muscle activity. Physical therapy. 2, 161-168

Chapter 7:

1. Benefits of Sunlight: A Bright Spot for Human HealthM. Nathaniel Mead Environ Health Perspect. 2008 Apr; 116(4): A160–A167.

2. Effects of exercise with or without light exposure on sleep quality and hormone reponsesHayan Lee, Sunho Kim, Donghee KimJ Exerc Nutrition Biochem. 2014 Sep; 18(3): 293–299. Published online 2014 Sep 11. doi: 10.5717/jenb.2014.18.3.293

3. Kowler E. Eye movements: The past 25 years. *Vision research.* 2011;51(13):1457-1483. doi:10.1016/j.visres.2010.12.014.

4. Saccadic eye movements in Parkinson's diseaseAnshul Srivastava, Ratna Sharma, Sanjay K Sood, Garima Shukla, Vinay Goyal, Madhuri Behari

   Indian J Ophthalmol. 2014 May; 62(5): 538–544. doi: 10.4103/0301-4738.133482

5. Gap Effect Abnormalities during a Visually Guided Pro-Saccade Task in Children with Attention Deficit Hyperactivity Disorder Yuka Matsuo, Masayuki Watanabe, Masako Taniike, Ikuko Mohri, Syoji Kobashi, Masaya Tachibana, Yasushi Kobayashi, Yuri KitamuraPLoS One. 2015; 10(5): e0125573. Published online 2015 May 27. doi: 10.1371/journal.pone.0125573

6. Kowler E. Eye movements: The past 25 years. *Vision research*. 2011;51(13):1457-1483. doi:10.1016/j.visres.2010.12.014.

7. Pinkhardt EH, Jürgens R, Lulé D, et al. Eye movement impairments in Parkinson's disease: possible role of extradopaminergic mechanisms. *BMC Neurology*. 2012;12:5. doi:10.1186/1471-2377-12-5.

8. Kim S, Kim S, Khalid A, et al. Rhythmical Photic Stimulation at Alpha Frequencies Produces Antidepressant-Like Effects in a Mouse Model of Depression. Svenningsson P, ed. *PLoS ONE*. 2016;11(1):e0145374. doi:10.1371/journal.pone.0145374.

9. Keeley PW, Reese BE. Morphology of Dopaminergic Amacrine Cells in the Mouse Retina: Independence from Homotypic Interactions. *The Journal of comparative neurology*. 2010;518(8):1220-1231. doi:10.1002/cne.22270.

10. Krauzlis RJ, Goffart L, Hafed ZM. Neuronal control of fixation and fixational eye movements. *Philosophical Transactions of the Royal Society B: Biological Sciences*. 2017;372(1718):20160205. doi:10.1098/rstb.2016.0205.

Chapter 8

1. Kohrt WM, Barry DW, Schwartz RS. Muscle Forces or Gravity: What Predominates Mechanical Loading on Bone? *Medicine and science in sports and exercise*. 2009;41(11):2050-2055. doi:10.1249/MSS.0b013e3181a8c717.

2. Merzenich MM, Van Vleet TM, Nahum M. Brain plasticity-based therapeutics. *Frontiers in Human Neuroscience.* 2014;8:385. doi:10.3389/fnhum.2014.00385

3. Mellilo, Robert. Disconnected Kids: New York: Penguin Group. 2009

4. Kharrazian Datis, Underground Wellness. (2014 Oct. 18) Retrieved from https://www.youtube.com/watch?v=-8nh1WAac34

5. Shu-Zhen Wang, Sha Li, Xiao-Yang Xu, Gui-Ping Lin, Li Shao, Yan Zhao, and Ting Huai Wang.

    Effect of slow abdominal breathing combined with biofeedback on blood pressure and heart rate variability in prehypertension. The Journal of Alternative and Complementary Medicine. October 2010, 16(10): 1039-1045. Doi: 10.1089/acm2009.0577

6. Dinoff A, Herrmann N, Swardfager W, et al. The Effect of Exercise Training on Resting Concentrations of Peripheral Brain-Derived Neurotrophic Factor (BDNF): A Meta-Analysis. Hills RK, ed. *PLoS ONE.* 2016;11(9):e0163037. doi:10.1371/journal.pone.0163037.

Chapter 11

1. Merzenich MM, Van Vleet TM, Nahum M. Brain plasticity-based therapeutics. *Frontiers in Human Neuroscience.* 2014;8:385. doi:10.3389/fnhum.2014.00385